D0461028

BELARUS

BELARUS

THEN & NOW

Prepared by
Geography Department

Lerner Publications Company
Minneapolis

Series editors: Mary M. Rodgers, Tom Streissguth,
  Colleen Sexton
Photo researcher: Bill Kauffmann
Designer: Zachary Marell

Our thanks to the following for their help in preparing
and checking the text of this book: Dr. Craig ZumBrun-
nen, Department of Geography, University of Washington;
and Father Anthony Ugolnik.

Pronunciation Guide

Bialystok	bee-AHL-ih-stok
Bug	BOOG
Gediminas	ged-ih-MIN-ahs
glasnost	GLAZ-nost
Mozyr	MOH-zer
narodny sud	nah-ROHD-nee SOOD
Polotsk	POH-lotsk
Pravoslavnii	prah-voh-SLAV-nee
Pripet	PRIHP-et
psalmniki	SAHLM-nee-kee
Vitebsk	vee-TEPSK
Wladyslaw	vlah-DIS-laff
Jagiello	yahg-YELL-lo
Zhlobin	jlo-BYIN

Terms in **bold** appear in a glossary that starts on page 52.

LIBRARY OF CONGRESS CATALOGING-IN-PUBLICATION DATA

Belarus / prepared by Geography Department, Lerner Publica-
  tions Company.
    p. cm. — (Then & now)
  Includes index.
  Summary: Discusses the history, geography, ethnic mixture,
politics, economy, and future of the former Soviet republic of
Belarus.
  ISBN 0-8225-2811-8 (lib. bdg.)
  1. Belarus—Juvenile literature. 2. Belarusians—Juvenile
literature. [1. Belarus.] I. Lerner Publications Company.
Geography Dept. II. Series: Then & now (Minneapolis, Minn.)
DK507.56.B45 1993
947'.65—dc20   92-33231
                                                        CIP
                                                         AC

Manufactured in the United States of America
1 2 3 4 5 6 98 97 96 95 94 93

• CONTENTS •

Young boys buy movie tickets in Minsk, the capital of Belarus.

"Until recently, [Soviet Byelorussia] seemed so stable, sensible, and reliable. Now passions are red hot."

The Newspaper Pravda, April 1991

In 1992, the Soviet Union would have celebrated the 75th anniversary of the revolution of 1917. During that revolt, political activists called **Communists** overthrew the czar (ruler) and the government of the **Russian Empire.** The revolution of 1917 was the first step in establishing the 15-member **Union of Soviet Socialist Republics (USSR).**

The Soviet Union stretched from eastern Europe across northern Asia and contained nearly 300 million people. Within this vast nation, the Communist government guaranteed housing, education, health care, and lifetime employment. Communist leaders told farmers and factory workers that Soviet citizens owned all property in common. The new nation quickly **industrialized,** meaning it built many new factories and upgraded existing ones. It also modernized and enlarged its farms. In addition, the USSR created a huge, well-equipped military force that allowed it to become one of the most powerful nations in the world.

A soldier leaves flowers at the foot of a war memorial in Minsk. About 80 percent of the city was destroyed during World War II (1939–1945).

The Byelorussian Soviet Socialist Republic, located in the western USSR, had become part of the Soviet Union in 1922. In the 1930s, while many other republics industrialized, **Soviet Byelorussia** maintained an economy largely based on agriculture. The region suffered great destruction and loss of life during two world wars in the 20th century. In addition, the harsh measures taken by Soviet leaders to **Russify** Byelorussia turned many **ethnic Belarussians** against Communist rule.

By the early 1990s, the Soviet Union was in a period of rapid change and turmoil. The central government had mismanaged the economy, which was failing to provide goods. To control the various ethnic groups within the USSR, the Communists had long restricted many freedoms. People throughout the vast nation, including many Belarussians, were dissatisfied.

Several of the republics were seeking independence from Soviet rule—a development that worried some old-style Communists. In August 1991, these conservative Communists tried to use Soviet military power to overthrow Mikhail Gorbachev, the USSR's president. Belarussian workers took this opportunity to go on strike to demand change.

After the attempted overthrow of Gorbachev failed, Soviet Byelorussia declared its independence and changed its name to Belarus. Within a few months, Minsk—the capital of Belarus—became the political seat of the **Commonwealth of Independent States**, a confederation of former Soviet republics. Commonwealth members are developing economic alliances, but ethnic strife unleashed by the breakup of the USSR threatens the future of the union.

Although Belarussian leaders have turned to other European nations for new investment, much of the country's economy depends on maintaining

Nuns chat outside an Eastern Orthodox church in the historic city of Polotsk. For more than 70 years, the Soviets restricted the Orthodox faith, which most Belarussians follow.

Belarus's red-and-white national flag flies over a government building in Brest, a southwestern city on the Polish border.

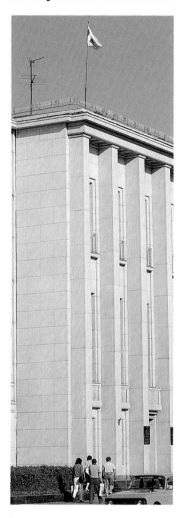

trade relations within the commonwealth. Belarus, for example, exchanges goods with the former Soviet republics of Russia and Ukraine. Road and rail links through the commonwealth will allow Belarussian companies access to markets in western Europe. Yet, if the new alliance fails, Belarussians will have to create a self-sufficient economy.

Shortages of fuel and goods persist throughout the former Soviet Union. Here, Belarussians wait in a long line to buy gas.

CHAPTER ONE

The Land and People of Belarus

T he word *Belarus* means "white Russia" in the Belarussian language. Many theories exist as to why this color is part of the country's name. Some say that white refers to the snow that often blankets Belarus or to the chalk-colored bark of the nation's many birch trees. In the literature and folklore of Belarus, white symbolizes freedom.

Belarus lacks natural barriers, such as seas and mountain ranges. As a result, the country's borders have often changed—most recently after World War II (1939–1945). To the east of Belarus is Russia, the largest of the former Soviet republics, and to the south lies Ukraine. Because of their location, Slavic populations, and languages, Belarus, Ukraine, and Russia are often called the **East Slavic nations.**

East of Brest, a carpenter skillfully repairs the semicircular window of a local church. In many parts of the country, workers are restoring long-neglected buildings to their original use and appearance.

Dense forests and flat plains are common in southeastern Belarus.

To the northwest, Belarus shares a long border with Lithuania and a shorter frontier with Latvia. These two nations and Estonia, a country farther north, make up the **Baltic States.** Poland, one of the **West Slavic nations,** lies along the western border of Belarus. With an area of 80,154 square miles (207,599 square kilometers), Belarus is slightly smaller than Britain or the state of Kansas.

• *Topography and Climate* •

A landlocked and low-lying country, Belarus spreads over part of the north central European Plain. The nation contains thick forests, flat marshes, and vast, open fields.

Children make a wobbly pyramid on a beach near the Neman River. The waterway also flows through neighboring Lithuania, where it is called the Nemunas.

During the last Ice Age, about 10,000 years ago, glaciers (sheets of slow-moving ice) formed a ridge of low, rolling hills known as **moraines** that stretch across Belarus. This Belarussian Ridge, which averages 75 miles (121 km) wide and 500 to 1000 feet (152 to 305 meters) high, extends from the southwestern to the northeastern corner of the country. Melting glaciers also shaped the low moraines, boulders, and shallow lakes of the Neman and Polotsk lowlands in northern and western Belarus.

The country's highest point, at 1,135 feet (346 m), lies in the Minsk Upland of central Belarus. North and south of the Minsk Upland and the Belarussian Ridge, the land is flat and dotted with swamps. The Pripet Marshes in the south are thickly forested lowlands that straddle the border with Ukraine.

In southern Belarus, near the city of Pinsk, thick grasses and swamps are typical landscape features.

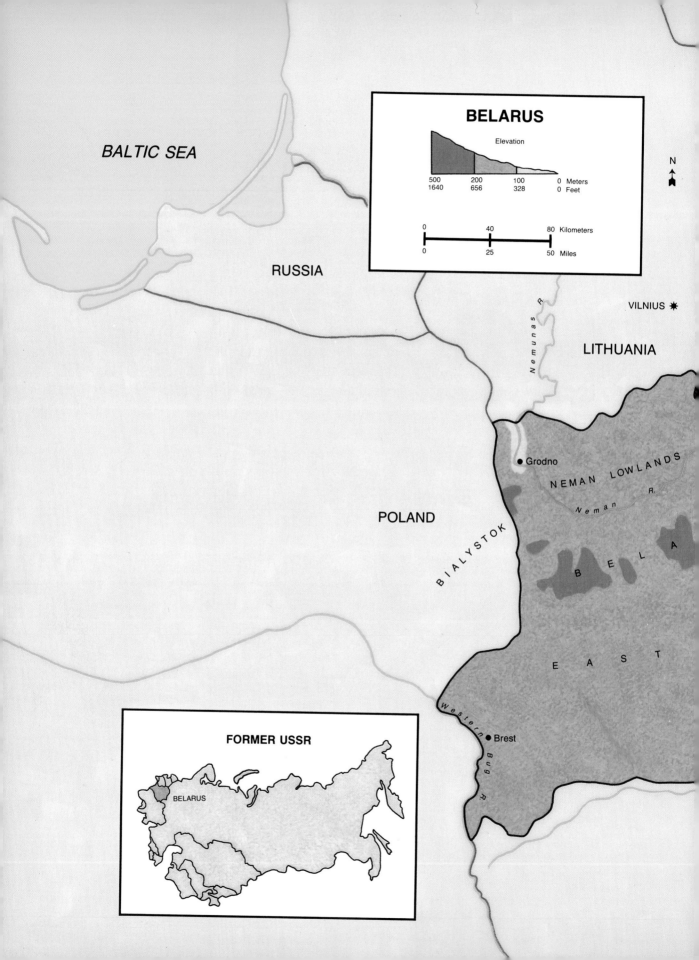

BALTIC SEA

RUSSIA

BELARUS

Elevation

| 500 | 200 | 100 | 0 | Meters |
| 1640 | 656 | 328 | 0 | Feet |

0   40   80   Kilometers

0   25   50   Miles

N

VILNIUS ✳

LITHUANIA

Nemunas R.

● Grodno

NEMAN LOWLANDS

Neman R.

B E L A

POLAND

B I A L Y S T O K

E A S T

Western Bug R.

● Brest

FORMER USSR

BELARUS

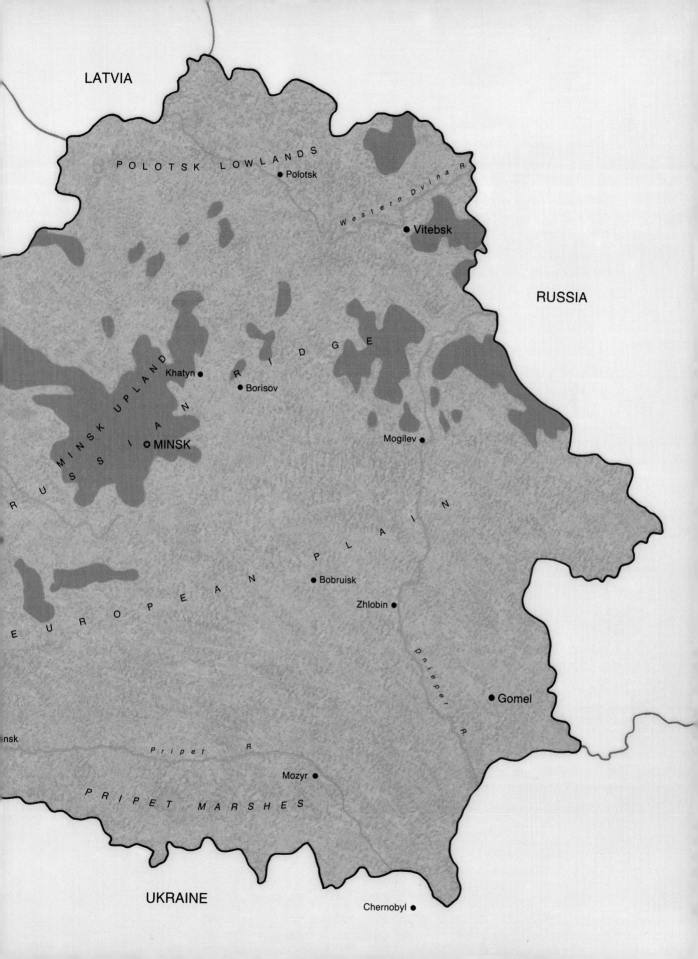

A man (right) *gazes at the waters of the Western Dvina River of northern Belarus. Children* (below) *swim in the Neman River that flows in the northwest.*

Lacking an outlet to the open sea or to any large body of water, Belarus has long depended on its rivers to ship its agricultural goods. Rivers north of the Belarussian Ridge flow northward to the Baltic Sea. South of the ridge, rivers run through Ukraine and eventually reach the Black Sea. These waterways freeze quickly in winter, however, and swamps line many of the riverbanks in low-lying regions.

The Dnieper River is the major waterway of eastern Belarus. The Western Bug forms part of Belarus's border with Poland. The Dnieper and the Western Bug are still used to transport lumber. The Neman River, which reaches the Baltic Sea, extends into Lithuania from northwestern Belarus. The Western Dvina River also flows in the north. The Pripet River rises in Ukraine, travels across the Pripet Marshes into Belarus, and joins the Dnieper on its way south to the Black Sea.

Compared to most of the former Soviet Union, Belarus has a moderate climate. Temperatures average 20° F (–7° C) in January, the coldest month, and 65° F (18° C) in July, the hottest month. Summer readings can exceed 90° F (32° C), but during much of the season the climate is mild and damp.

Winter weather can be severe, with deep snows and frigid gusts blowing from the east. Occasionally, warm westerly winds from the Baltic Sea moderate Belarus's winters. Eastern Belarus experiences the coldest winter temperatures. Annual average precipitation ranges from 20 to 36 inches (51 to 91 centimeters). Snow covers the ground for four months every year.

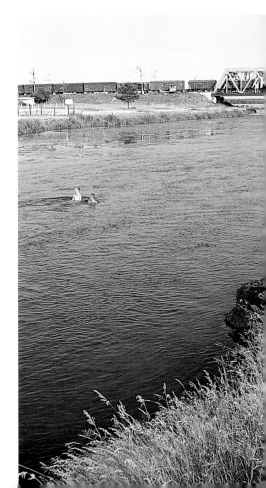

• *Cities* •

Two-thirds of Belarus's 10.3 million people live in cities. Most Belarussian towns were founded by the end of the 12th century. The northern city of Polotsk, the country's oldest settlement, dates to 862. Belarus suffered widespread destruction in World War I (1914–1918) and World War II, however, and most of the nation's historic urban architecture has been lost.

Minsk (population 1.6 million), the capital, lies in the rolling hills of central Belarus. An ancient trading center, Minsk has been invaded and destroyed many times in its history. Yet the city has benefited from its position along important road and rail routes that run east and west (between central Europe and Russia), and north and south (between the Baltic States and Ukraine).

Demolished by two world wars in the 20th century, Minsk has been rebuilt in an up-to-date style. This memorial to the victims of World War I (1914–1918) hangs over a clothing store.

Lights burn in a modern apartment complex in Minsk. More than 65 percent of all Belarussians live in urban areas.

In Vitebsk, young Belarussians repair the artwork in a local church.

The Soviet government rebuilt Minsk after World War II and established government offices, major businesses, universities, and scientific institutes in the city. Factories in Minsk produce tractors, farm machinery, and trucks for export. The printing industry is also important. Many small, private farms exist near Minsk, which processes vegetables and fruit for wide distribution.

With 506,000 people, Gomel is the second largest city in Belarus. Located in the southeast, Gomel produces agricultural machinery, fertilizers, machine tools, and river boats and barges. Vitebsk (population 356,000), which lies in the northeast along the Western Dvina River, is an important industrial center. The city has machine and metal industries, as well as wood-processing complexes and textile plants. Mogilev (population 363,000) is a hub for barge traffic along the Dnieper River. Ancient landmarks in Mogilev include old churches and a defensive tower.

Brest (population 269,000), a historic fortified city, lies near the Western Bug River along the border between Belarus and Poland. Workers in Brest and in the city of Grodno, also near the Polish border, are employed in light manufacturing and food-processing industries. The cities of Bobruisk and Borisov, in central Belarus, have sawmills and light industries.

• Ethnic Heritage •

Because of its unstable borders and frequent domination by foreigners, Belarus contains many different ethnic groups. Poles, Lithuanians, and Russians have claimed Belarussian territory in the past. In general, these separate peoples have managed to live together peacefully, and Belarus has avoided the ethnic conflicts that mark other parts of central and eastern Europe.

Ethnic Belarussians make up 79 percent of the country's population. **Ethnic Russians**, most of whom live in urban areas, account for an additional 12 percent. Many ethnic Russians have moved to Belarus since 1945. In the west live ethnic Poles, and ethnic Ukrainians have settled mostly in the south.

At a kindergarten in Brest, students (above) *exercise with balls. An elderly Belarussian* (below) *sweeps the street with a handmade broom.*

Before World War II, about 10 percent of the Belarussian people were Jews. Historically, most Belarussians were farmers, and the country's Polish and Jewish minorities were businesspeople. During World War II, when Germany fought the USSR, the invading Germans arrested, tortured, and murdered Jews in Belarus. After the war, the Soviet government passed strict measures limiting religious practice. The Jewish culture of Belarus never recovered from these harsh events, and many Belarussian Jews are now resettling in Israel, a nation in the Middle East.

• *Language and Religion* •

Belarussians speak their own language, which has been an important mark of identity for the country's people. Closely related to Russian and Ukrainian, Belarussian also contains words from Old Slavonic, the ancestor of these modern Slavic languages. Although Belarussian has several dialects, writers and educators now use a standard literary form of the language in their books and classrooms.

The use of Belarussian declined while the country was part of the Soviet Union. The Soviet government forced Belarussian students to learn Russian, and by 1991 many young Belarussians no longer knew the language of their own country. Through broadcasts and language courses, Belarussians are

Street signs in Minsk appear in both the Russian and Belarussian languages.

An artist in a 19th-century church in Vitebsk carefully pens religious text using Cyrillic—the alphabet with which Belarussian, Russian, and Ukrainian are written.

now attempting to restore the national language to their schools and legal system.

Religion is also an important part of Belarussian culture. Some ancient, pre-Christian practices have survived in Belarus, which was one of the last European regions to adopt Christianity. For example, some Belarussians chant spells to ward off disease or to bring good fortune. Belarussians still tell *kazki*, satirical moral stories, and sing *psalmniki*, lively spiritual songs.

Despite attempts to suppress religion under the former Soviet government, Belarussians had a reputation for strong religious belief. The majority of people in Belarus still belong to the Eastern Orthodox Church, which is also the dominant faith in Russia and Ukraine. The Belarussian name for this faith

Once ruled by Catholic Poland, Belarus has an active Roman Catholic population. Believers place flowers at streetside shrines (top) *and attend Mass in restored churches* (below).

The stained-glass window (right) *of a physics lab at Minsk State University includes the nuclear equation E=mc², which the scientist Albert Einstein developed in the early 20th century. Undergraduates* (below) *listen to a physics lecture in one of the university's halls.*

—*Pravoslavnii,* meaning "right praising"—underlines the importance of song in the life of Orthodox Belarussians.

A large minority of people in Belarus are Roman Catholic, a fact that reflects the long years of rule by Poland, a Catholic nation. During the history of Belarus, its foreign rulers used religious loyalty to strengthen their control of the region. Catholic Belarussians, for example, were considered to be "Polish," whereas Orthodox Belarussians were seen as "Russian." Although the Soviets imposed controls on both faiths, Eastern Orthodox and Roman Catholic Christians now worship freely.

• Education and Health •

The Belarussian government provides free education from preschool through postsecondary levels. Primary school lasts about nine years. For two or three more years, students attend secondary schools, many of which teach trade skills. The University of Minsk and the Academy of Sciences are the major institutions of higher learning. Other schools offer courses in agricultural, technical, or language skills. Belarus has also opened several schools of theology (the study of religion).

Under Soviet rule, new clinics and hospitals were built in Belarus, and the state supported an extensive health-care system. But independence has brought economic problems that have led to a

shortage of medicines, of modern equipment, and of trained personnel. The average life expectancy in Belarus is 72 years. Infant mortality—the number of babies who die before they are one year old—is 20 per 1,000 live births.

Belarus also must care for thousands of patients who are suffering from the effects of an accident at the nuclear power plant in Chernobyl, Ukraine. In 1986, an explosion and fire at the plant released massive amounts of **radiation** into the air. The accident caused radiation ailments in 2,000,000 Belarussians, including 500,000 children. Many residents were evacuated from their homes, and a large area of southern Belarus is still considered unsafe.

The Belarussian government pays for most types of medical care, including dental work.

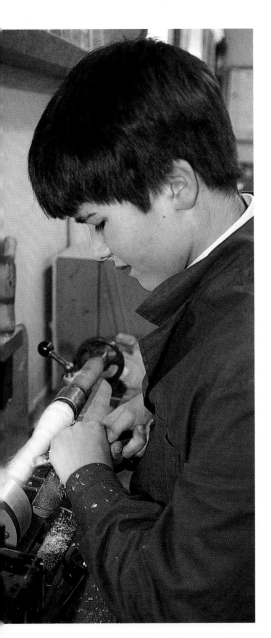

A student operates a woodcarving instrument during technical-training classes at his secondary school.

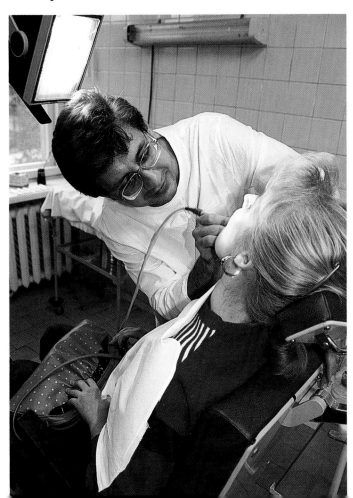

CHAPTER TWO

Belarus's Story

A land with few physical barriers, Belarus has often been at the crossroads of war and invasion. Throughout the country's history, foreign rulers have tried to convince the Belarussians that they were Poles or Russians or Lithuanians. But a distinct Belarussian culture survived through centuries of domination by neighboring powers.

Archaeologists have uncovered settlements from the Neolithic period (beginning about 10,000 B.C.) in the areas of Vitebsk and Minsk. By the 5th century B.C., early Belarussians were settling in the forests and low-lying plains near the Pripet River. These people built small, self-sufficient villages in remote locations to ensure their safety from invaders.

Gradually, a closely knit social organization known as the *zadruga,* or joint-family system, took shape. Married couples lived under the authority

During World War II, the occupying Germans massacred the inhabitants of Khatyn, a village that lies north of Minsk, and burned their cottages. The Soviets later reconstructed the site as a war memorial. This wall in the Khatyn Memorial commemorates Belarussians who died in German concentration camps.

of an elected leader. Wealth was determined by labor, and women had strong legal and property rights. The early Belarussians also maintained an independent form of justice, in which villagers chose their own judges. During centuries of foreign domination, the Belarussians used the *narodny sud*— or courts of custom—to bypass the justice systems of outside rulers.

• *The Nation in the Making* •

In the 6th century A.D., nomadic Slavic peoples from central Asia moved westward into the European Plain. The Slavs eventually settled in central, southern, and eastern Europe. The first rulers of Rus—the nation of the eastern Slavs—were Scandinavian Vikings who used the area's rivers to trade in eastern and northern Europe.

The Viking warrior Rurik, who died in A.D. 879, made the Slavic trading cities of Novgorod (now in Russia) and Kiev (now in Ukraine) part of Rus. His descendant Prince Vladimir forced the Slavs of Rus to convert to the Orthodox (or Eastern) branch of Christianity in 988. Kiev became the center of the eastern Slavic lands. After Vladimir's death in 1015, however, Kiev's princes divided the nation into principalities (realms of princes).

Belarus has its origins in the Principality of Polotsk, a city in the northern part of the country. Although Polotsk was a political and religious hub, many independent princes ruled the surrounding

Onion-shaped domes are characteristic of Eastern Orthodox churches. Orthodox Christianity, which by the 10th century dominated most areas of eastern Europe, differed from the Roman Catholic faith that was followed in western Europe. By the mid-11th century, the Orthodox and Roman churches had formally split.

In the 13th century, the Tatar chief Batu Khan conquered Rus, a kingdom that included the territory of modern Belarus.

area. In 1240, **Tatars** from central Asia invaded Kiev and the smaller settlement of Moscow (now in Russia). At the same time, the **Order of Teutonic Knights**—a Catholic German army—was conquering lands along the Baltic Sea to the north.

• The Foundations of Litva •

To resist these hostile forces, the princes of Belarus allied with the Lithuanians, who were fighting both the Poles and the Teutonic knights. In the 13th century, the Lithuanians and the Belarussians formed **Litva**, a state the Lithuanians called the Grand Duchy of Lithuania.

Gediminas, the grand duke of Lithuania from 1316 to 1341, also ruled lands in Belarus, Ukraine, and Poland. During his reign, a Christian military organization called the Order of Teutonic Knights repeatedly offered him baptism into the Christian faith. Gediminas refused to convert—a decision that caused frequent clashes between the grand duke's forces and the knights.

Vytautas the Great, a descendant of Gediminas, defeated the Teutonic knights at the Battle of Tannenberg in 1410.

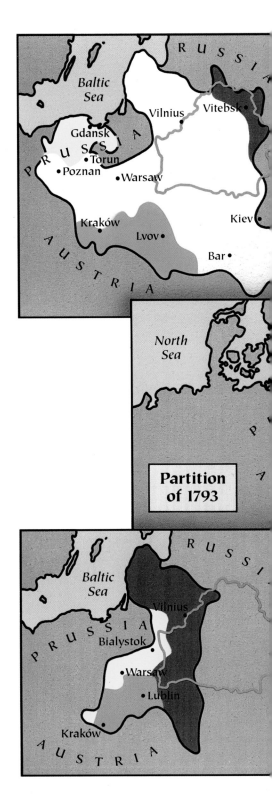

Partition of 1793

In 1323, Grand Duke Gediminas moved Litva's seat of government to Vilnius, the capital of modern Lithuania. By siding with their neighbors, however, Belarussian leaders gradually lost control of their own realm. In 1386, Grand Duke Jogaila of Litva also became, by marriage, Wladyslaw II Jageillo, the king of Poland. Although Jogaila converted to Roman Catholicism—the faith of the Poles—the Lithuanians and Belarussians resisted the new religion.

Vytautas, the cousin of Jogaila, defeated the Teutonic knights in 1410 at the Battle of Tannenberg. Under Vytautas, Litva expanded from the Baltic Sea south to the Black Sea, and from Poland eastward nearly to Moscow. With one of the strongest armies in Europe, Litva was able to prevent the Tatars from reaching western Europe.

**Russian Partitions
(late 1700s)**

Polish-Lithuanian
Commonwealth

To Prussia

To Russia

To Austria

Current border
of Belarus

**Partition
of 1772**

**Partition
of 1795**

Miles
0 50 100   200

0   100 200
Kilometers

• Poland and Russia •

In 1569, Poland tightened its control over the region by forming the Union of Lublin, which established the Polish-Lithuanian Commonwealth. **Polonization,** or the introduction of the Polish language and of Polish customs, soon followed. The nobles of Litva also accepted Polish nationality. The Union of Brest in 1596 imposed a religious alliance with the Roman Catholic Church upon the Orthodox Belarussians. Despite Polonization, the Belarussian language and culture remained strong.

The leaders of the Polish-Lithuanian Commonwealth faced the expansion of the Russian Empire, a realm centered in Moscow, during the 1600s and 1700s. Litva became a battleground between Poland and Russia, a development that weakened the commonwealth. Between 1772 and 1795, Russia enforced three partitions (divisions) of the Polish-Lithuanian Commonwealth. These partitions eliminated Poland as a state and put the Belarussian lands of Litva under Russian control. The Belarussians exchanged their Polish king for a Russian czar (ruler).

• Rebellion and Resistance •

Under Russian rule, Belarus lost much of its identity. In 1840, for example, Czar Nicholas I prohibited the use of the name Belarus. The Belarussian peasants became **serfs** who were tied to the

In the 17th and 18th centuries, Belarus was part of the Polish-Lithuanian Commonwealth. During that time, armies of the Russian Empire attacked the region. Russia eventually defeated the commonwealth's troops and enforced three separate partitions (divisions) of its territory. By 1795, Belarussian lands were under Russian control.

A cartoon (below) *shows wealthy Russian landowners gambling with the lives of their serfs (landless farm workers). The patched clothing of a Russian peasant* (right) *reveals the poverty in which most of the empire's population lived.*

land and who labored for the benefit of distant Russian landowners. Although Czar Alexander II freed the serfs in 1861, most of them remained poor, illiterate, and landless.

In 1863, 75,000 peasants, as well as some Belarussian nobles, joined a violent rebellion. Their leader, Kostus Kalinouski, demanded independence for Belarus. The revolt failed, and Kalinouski was captured. After his execution, he became a symbol of the Belarussian struggle against Russian rule.

In reaction to the uprising, Russia enforced its policies even more harshly. Nevertheless, in the 1870s and 1880s, a new movement for freedom spread across the Russian Empire. Educated young people moved to villages and tried to join the peasants in living a country life. This idealistic movement eventually fell apart, but it kindled a widespread desire for reform. By the early 1900s, Belarussian social democrats, who opposed czarist rule and sought a written constitution, were demanding an independent state in Belarus.

• *Revolution and War* •

In the early 20th century, Belarus was one of the poorest areas of Europe. Peasants, who made up 86 percent of the population, paid heavy taxes to their rulers and lived on farms averaging less than 20 acres (8 hectares) in size. Belarus also had the highest illiteracy rate in Europe. These conditions prompted many people to move abroad. Between 1885 and 1915, nearly 1,000,000 Belarussians emigrated to the United States, and more than 500,000 settled new lands in Siberia, a distant region of the Russian Empire.

In 1905, a violent protest broke out in Russia. Strikes and street demonstrations took place in Moscow and in St. Petersburg, the empire's capital. This revolt also sparked a nationalist revival in Belarus. Belarussian writers—including the poets Ianka Kupala and Iakub Kolas—described the suffering and the hopes of their people. The Belarussian Hramada (group) drew up a nationalist political

Modern Belarussians leave flowers to honor the nationalist leaders Ianka Kupala and Iakub Kolas. Kupala, whose real name was Ivan Lutsevich, wrote poetry and translated Russian novels into Belarussian. Kolas, the pseudonym of Konstantin Mitskevich, lived most of his life in Minsk, where he authored classic works in the Belarussian language.

program and inspired advances in education. For the first time, Belarussian peasants began to enroll in schools. Although the 1905 revolt failed, the Belarussians continued to demand independence.

The independence movement remained active, even during World War I. In this conflict, German and Russian armies fought fierce battles that caused widespread destruction. The defeat of the Russian forces led to growing discontent within the empire. Soldiers mutinied, and workers walked off their jobs in protest of low wages. A rebellion in St. Petersburg in March 1917 led to the fall of the czar.

In October, revolutionaries known as Communists overthrew the Russian government. Belarussian leaders proclaimed an independent republic in March 1918, but the Communists quickly defeated this state and established control in 1919. Two years later, Poland **annexed** (took over) a part of western Belarus. In 1922, Communist leaders added the Byelorussian Soviet Socialist Republic to the Union of Soviet Socialist Republics (USSR).

• *Soviet Rule and World War II* •

The new Soviet government took over banks, mines, and industries and put them under the control of government managers. Farmers were forced to join **collective farms,** on which all the laborers received a portion of the harvest as their wages. The Soviet government took possession of the farmers' land, buildings, and machinery.

A statue at the Khatyn Memorial depicts a lone survivor of the Khatyn burning as he carries the body of a dead villager.

The Khatyn Memorial commemorates all Belarussians who died during the German occupation. This field of urns is a reminder of more than 100 other villages in Belarus that, like Khatyn, were entirely destroyed.

In the 1930s, the regime of Adolf Hitler in Germany began preparing for another war in Europe. Hitler signed the **Molotov-Ribbentrop Pact** with Joseph Stalin, the Soviet leader, in 1939. According to the agreement, Stalin and Hitler would share control of Poland, with eastern Poland going to the Soviet Union. In September, the German and Soviet armies invaded Poland. Lands annexed by Poland in 1921 were returned to Soviet Byelorussia. These actions drew several western European nations into World War II.

Two years later, in June 1941, Hitler ordered a surprise attack on the Soviet Union. The unprepared Soviet army quickly retreated. The Germans marched almost unopposed through Soviet Byelorussia and subjected the region to a brutal occupation. Although the Soviet Union defeated the Germans in 1945, more than 70 percent of all buildings in Soviet Byelorussia had been leveled. Minsk, the largest city in the republic, was almost completely destroyed.

• *The Road to Independence* •

In 1945, a treaty between the Soviet Union and Poland established the present boundaries of Belarus. A Communist government and a Communist economic system were established in Poland. The Bialystok region that once had been part of Soviet Byelorussia became Polish territory. This division has since caused tensions between Bialystok's Orthodox and Catholic populations.

Within Soviet Byelorussia, Stalin's regime limited the use of the Belarussian language and executed teachers, scholars, and religious leaders who opposed Soviet rule. The process of Russification deprived Belarus and other Soviet republics of their political and cultural independence.

The Soviets did allow Belarus and Ukraine to become members of the **United Nations** (UN). By this action, the Soviet Union gained additional UN voting power. Within Soviet Byelorussia, however, ethnic Belarussians made up a minority of the republic's leaders and administrators. Russians in search of jobs moved into Belarussian cities, and the Soviet government deported Belarussians to Russia and to Soviet central Asia.

• *The New Era* •

The rapid expansion of industry and a program of rebuilding after World War II benefited Soviet Byelorussia through the 1960s and 1970s. By the 1980s, however, the USSR's economy was in decline. Factories were producing shoddy goods, and food shortages were making life difficult for average workers. In 1985, Mikhail Gorbachev became the Soviet leader and introduced a policy of *glasnost* (meaning "openness" in Russian). By allowing public criticism, Gorbachev sought to improve the inefficient Communist system.

A *wall painting shows Soviet citizens marching forward into the future. The famous symbols of Soviet Communism—the hammer and the sickle—are also prominent.*

The people of Soviet Byelorussia took the opportunity to demand more local control of their own affairs. In 1986, Belarussians also protested the government's actions during the accident at the Chernobyl nuclear station. Soviet officials waited several days to warn residents of the danger of radioactivity, which had poisoned huge areas of cropland and hundreds of thousands of people.

In several nations of eastern Europe, including Poland, Communist governments were falling from power. But the movement for complete independence from the Soviet Union grew slowly in Belarus. Many Belarussians feared that their close economic ties with the USSR made self-rule unwise. Yet, in April 1991, thousands of Belarussian factory laborers and transportation workers went on strike to protest rising prices. The strikers demanded the resignation of Gorbachev and more independence for Belarus.

Several other Soviet republics were also seeking control over their own economies and administrations. Gorbachev responded by proposing a new treaty that would give the republics greater self-government. Conservative Communists saw the treaty as a threat to their power, and on August 19, 1991, a group of Soviet officials arrested Gorbachev. By overthrowing Gorbachev in a **coup d'état**, they sought to restore central control over the Soviet republics.

In 1991, *Belarussian strikers* (left) *blocked railroad traffic in an attempt to force authorities in Soviet Byelorussia (now Belarus) to control rising prices.*

In several Soviet cities, including Moscow, people marched in the streets to express their opposition to the coup. After a few days, the attempted overthrow failed, and the Soviet Union began to break apart. Within a week, Belarus became the 6th republic to withdraw from the Soviet Union. The UN delegate from Belarus now represented an independent Belarussian government.

The Belarussian gymnast Vitaly Shcherbo won a record six gold medals at the 1992 summer Olympic Games in Barcelona, Spain. Here, he finishes his routine on the parallel bars.

Belarus declared its independence from Soviet rule in August 1991. Former Soviet soldiers, however, continue to reside in the new country.

(Left) **A shrine at Belarus's border with Lithuania honors people killed during the struggle for independence.** (Below) **The founding members of the Commonwealth of Independent States chose this building in Minsk as their headquarters.**

• Independence •

The Soviet government had left behind a system in which the republics could not produce enough goods for their own populations. Although Belarus and other republics were independent, their leaders saw the need for continued economic and political cooperation. On December 8, 1991, Russia, Ukraine, and Belarus established the Commonwealth of Independent States, with Minsk as its capital. Several other Soviet republics have joined the commonwealth, which has become a loose economic and military association.

Although many of the former Soviet republics are experiencing political turmoil, Belarus has remained peaceful under the country's new leader, Stanislav Shushkevich. But Belarussians still face serious economic problems. Without Soviet control of prices and distribution, the cost of living in Belarus has risen and some goods are in short supply. To make the country's factories more efficient, the Belarussian government is allowing obsolete industries to fail and close down. As a result, many Belarussian workers are losing their jobs.

To help its economy, Belarus has established commercial ties with foreign nations, including Poland and other former Communist countries of eastern Europe. Belarussians are also seeking **joint ventures,** or partnerships, with international businesses. The example of Poland—and of other European countries that recently have transformed their economies—may help the Belarussians to set a successful future course.

CHAPTER THREE

Making a Living in Belarus

Under centralized Soviet rule, Belarus had little control over its own industries and resources. Most of the goods manufactured in Belarussian factories were delivered to Russia and to other Soviet republics. Government agencies planned the production of food, machinery, energy, and other important goods. The Soviets guaranteed employment and set consumer prices. Central planning, however, left Belarus unprepared for a free-market system, in which businesses fail if they cannot sell their products or services.

With the fall of the Soviet government, the central planning system has ended. Having gained their political independence, Belarussians must now update their factories and seek new foreign markets for their products. President Shushkevich supports a rapid change to a free-market economy, despite the risk that this move will cause unemployment, shortages, and price increases.

Farm equipment is one of Belarus's chief industrial products. Factories in Minsk assemble tractors for export to many foreign countries, as well as to former Soviet republics.

• Agriculture and Forestry •

The economy of Belarus has traditionally been based on the country's abundant natural resources, including fertile soil and extensive forests. More than one-third of Belarussian land is under cultivation, and another one-third is forested.

The cool climate and dense soil of Belarus are well suited to fodder crops, which support herds of cattle and pigs. Root crops, such as sugar beets and potatoes, are also important. Farmers in northern Belarus grow flax, a crop that yields natural fibers used to make linen and other textiles. Nearly 20 percent of Belarus's productive soil, however, was contaminated by radiation from the Chernobyl accident, and in some areas crop growing has ceased altogether.

The Belarussian government hopes to break up the collective farms established under Soviet rule and to return the land to private ownership. This

After gathering wheat, farmers near Grodno use machinery to turn and dry the grain.

change will allow farmers to sell their produce at a profit. The government of Belarus also plans to transfer food-processing industries to private owners.

The Belarussian forests have suffered from poor management. Under the Soviet administration, trees were cut down at a faster rate than they were planted. The new government of Belarus intends to give closer attention to forestry, because sawmills provide the essential raw materials for furniture, plywood, and other important products.

Severe shortages of food and timber in neighboring republics may also help the Belarussian food- and timber-processing industries. The country will be able to market many of its products in Europe—provided they are free from radiation.

East of Brest, a large sawmill makes building materials from wood that was recently logged in the forests of southern Belarus.

Crews load freshly harvested potatoes into bins before shipping them to markets in Vitebsk.

FATAL FALLOUT IN BELARUS

In April 1986, an explosion rocked the nuclear power plant at Chernobyl in northern Ukraine. The station's fuel core overheated and released more than 11 tons (10 metric tons) of **radiation** into the air. Winds carried 70 percent of the invisible and dangerous particles—called fallout—to Belarus.

The fallout poisoned much of the country's soil and infected many Belarussians, especially children, with cancer and other illnesses. Since the explosion, Belarussian doctors have treated more cases of thyroid cancer, stomach diseases, and breathing ailments.

Eighteen percent of the soil on Belarus's farms is now unsafe for growing crops. To meet rising demands for food, however, Belarussian farmers continue to raise vegetables, fruits and livestock in this unsafe soil. Although villagers have been warned about the dangers of eating food from their gardens, many of them depend on this produce to feed their families.

During the disaster, the Soviet government was slow to inform the public about the dangers of the nuclear accident. Many Belarussians continued to inhabit homes and villages poisoned by radiation. After Belarus gained independence from Soviet rule, the country's officials began to take action to protect their citizens by monitoring radiation levels and by evacuating contaminated villages. In addition, the government built new clinics that specialize in treating radiation poisoning. Belarus's leaders and scientists have also promised to use their new freedom to educate the world about the hazards of unsafe nuclear power plants.

Belarussians gather to mourn those who have died from radiation sickness.

• Manufacturing •

Although more than half of Belarus's income comes from manufacturing, inefficiency has hurt the country's industries. Many factories cannot obtain the parts needed to make finished goods, such as motorcycles, ball bearings, plywood, and linens. The new government is trying to improve the supply system and to convert the factories to private ownership. Plant managers, instead of government planners, now oversee the manufacture and distribution of industrial goods.

Soviet Byelorussia once led the USSR in the production of heavy trucks and harvesters, and Belarussian tractors powered much of Soviet agriculture. Belarus still exports farm machinery to the former Soviet republics and to the United States. New factories make electronic instruments and computers. Electronics made in Belarus are the best among the former Soviet republics but are not yet competitive on the world market.

Food-processing plants in Belarus prepare canned meats, fruits, and vegetables. Textile factories exist in Minsk and Vitebsk. In the 1980s, the country built its first steel mill at Zhlobin. Glassmaking is also an important activity in Belarus, although this industry is suffering from a shortage of raw materials.

• Energy •

Belarus was long thought to lack petroleum resources. In the south, however, geologists have found reserves of high-quality coal, natural gas, and petroleum. The country also contains oil shale, a rock from which oil can be extracted. Belarus can no longer buy oil supplies cheaply from Russia, so having its own energy reserves has become important to the national economy.

Stone from eastern Belarus is the raw material for this brick factory in the capital.

Although these workers are assembling tractor gearboxes by hand, most Belarussian plants are highly mechanized operations that include robots and computers.

Oil and gas pipelines crisscross Belarus, allowing the country to use these fuels or to charge fees for transporting the fuels elsewhere. This natural gas pipeline operates in southern Belarus.

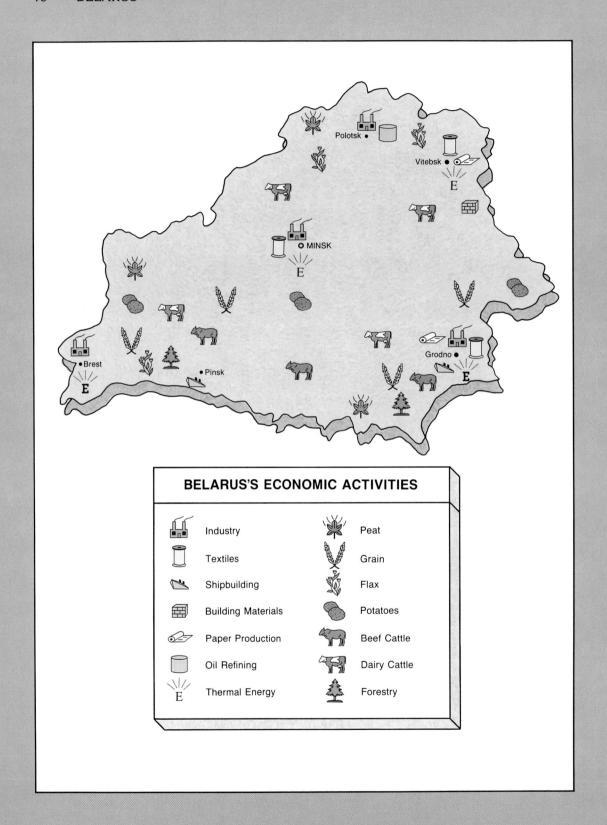

BELARUS'S ECONOMIC ACTIVITIES

Industry		Peat	
Textiles		Grain	
Shipbuilding		Flax	
Building Materials		Potatoes	
Paper Production		Beef Cattle	
Oil Refining		Dairy Cattle	
Thermal Energy		Forestry	

Boats bob outside a plant that produces electricity using the power of steam and heated water.

Belarus does control an important pipeline through which Russia pumps its oil westward to central Europe. Along this pipeline, Belarussian refineries at Polotsk and Mozyr process the crude oil for fuel. The Polotsk refinery also provides the raw material to make fertilizer, plastics, and artificial fibers.

Geothermal plants, which use heated underground water to drive generators, exist in western Belarus. Most industry, however, is powered by burning **peat**, which is densely compressed ancient vegetation. Belarus contains huge quantities of peat, a smoky but reliable source of energy.

The Soviets promoted nuclear energy as an inexpensive source of fuel. Following the destructive accident at Chernobyl, many Belarussians became opposed to nuclear power. The nine power plants in Belarus meet less than one-third of the country's electricity demand.

CHAPTER FOUR

What's Next for Belarus?

O f all the former Soviet republics, Belarus has the closest cultural and political ties to Russia. In contrast to many regions of the Soviet Union, Belarus experienced a peaceful transition to self-government. The country has also avoided the ethnic conflicts that are troubling many nations of the old USSR. Most of the Russians who arrived during Soviet rule have chosen to remain in Belarus.

After the breakup of the Soviet government, Belarussian leaders cooperated with Russia and Ukraine in establishing the Commonwealth of Independent States. As one of the founding members of the commonwealth, Belarus has a strong voice in its future. In addition, Belarus's shortages of oil and natural gas—fuels possessed in abundance by Russia and Ukraine—is an important motive for Belarussians to remain active in the commonwealth.

Belarussians line up to buy fresh tomatoes. Shortages of food and consumer goods have made waiting in line part of everyday life in Belarus.

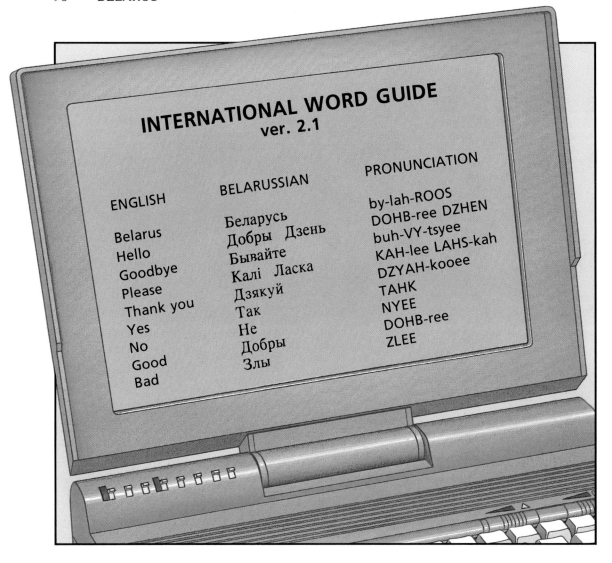

INTERNATIONAL WORD GUIDE
ver. 2.1

ENGLISH	BELARUSSIAN	PRONUNCIATION
Belarus	Беларусь	by-lah-ROOS
Hello	Добры Дзень	DOHB-ree DZHEN
Goodbye	Бывайте	buh-VY-tsyee
Please	Калі Ласка	KAH-lee LAHS-kah
Thank you	Дзякуй	DZYAH-kooee
Yes	Так	TAHK
No	Не	NYEE
Good	Добры	DOHB-ree
Bad	Злы	ZLEE

With its economic links to Russia and to more prosperous European countries, Belarus also has the opportunity to develop a successful open economy. Poland—a country to the west that also overthrew Communist rule—has made slow but steady economic progress. The Baltic States to the northwest have established joint ventures and have good ports and transportation links to the rest of northern Europe. If Belarus can take advantage of the growing markets in these neighboring nations, it has a chance to prosper.

Nevertheless, changing to a free-market system carries problems and risks. If companies are allowed to fail, many workers will suffer unemployment. If prices are allowed to rise freely without government controls, many Belarussians will be unable to afford consumer goods and food. Widespread unemployment and a low standard of living could bring conflict and could hamper the success of the government's new policies.

A woman in Polotsk raises cucumbers and other vegetables in a plot outside her home.

FAST FACTS ABOUT BELARUS

Total Population	10.3 million
Ethnic Mixture	79 percent Belarussian 12 percent Russian 4 percent Polish 2 percent Ukrainian
CAPITAL and Major Cities	MINSK, Gomel, Vitebsk, Mogilev, Brest, Grodno
Major Languages	Belarussian, Russian
Major Religion	Orthodox Christian
Year of inclusion in USSR	1922
Status	Fully independent state, founding member of Commonwealth of Independent States; member of United Nations since 1945 but changed name from Byelorussian SSR to Belarus in 1991

annex: to add a country or territory to the domain of another nation by force.

Baltic States: a common term for Estonia, Latvia, and Lithuania—independent nations that border the Baltic Sea to the northwest of Belarus.

collective farm: a large agricultural estate worked by a group. The workers usually received a portion of the farm's harvest as wages. On a Soviet collective farm, the central government owned the land, buildings, and machinery.

Commonwealth of Independent States: a union of former Soviet republics that was created by the leaders of Russia, Belarus, and Ukraine in December 1991. The commonwealth has no formal constitution and functions as a loose economic and military association.

Communist: a person who supports Communism—an economic system in which the government owns all farmland and the means of producing goods in factories.

coup d'état: French words meaning "blow to the state" that refer to a swift, sudden overthrow of a government.

East Slavic nation: one of the three nations—Belarus, Ukraine, and Russia—settled by Slavic peoples in eastern Europe.

ethnic Belarussian: a person whose heritage is Slavic and who speaks Belarussian.

While attending school, this 12-year-old student also learns carpentry skills.

A young Belarussian enjoys a glass of kvas, *a popular drink made from malt, flour, sugar, mint, and fruits.*

ethnic Russian: a person whose heritage is Slavic and who speaks Russian.

glasnost: a Russian word meaning "openness" that refers to a policy of easing restrictions on writing and speech.

industrialize: to build and modernize factories for the purpose of manufacturing a wide variety of consumer goods and machinery.

joint venture: an economic partnership between a locally owned business and a foreign-owned company.

Litva: the Belarussian name for a realm formed in the 13th century by Lithuanians and Belarussians.

Molotov-Ribbentrop Pact: an agreement negotiated by Vyacheslav Molotov of the Soviet Union and Joachim von Ribbentrop of Germany. Signed in 1939, the agreement said that the two nations would not attack one another or interfere with one another's military and political activities. The pact secretly allowed the Soviet Union to add eastern Poland to Soviet Byelorussia.

moraine: a long, low hill made up of glacial deposits of soil and rock.

Order of Teutonic Knights: a military brotherhood of German Christians that took over parts of Estonia and Latvia in the 1200s and 1300s.

peat: decayed vegetation that has become densely packed down in swamps and bogs. Peat can be cut, dried, and burned as fuel.

Polonization: to impose the Polish language and culture on a non-Polish population.

radiation: energy that can be used to produce electricity but that can be harmful if absorbed by the human body.

Russian Empire: a large kingdom that covered present-day Russia as well as areas to the west and south. It existed from roughly the mid-1500s to 1917.

Russify: to make Russian by imposing the Russian language and culture on non-Russian peoples.

serf: a rural worker under the feudal landowning system, which tied laborers to a farming estate for life. Serfs had few rights and owed their labor and a large portion of their harvest to the landowner.

Soviet Byelorussia: a republic that became a part of the USSR in 1922. After gaining independence in 1991, Soviet Byelorussia was renamed Belarus.

Tatar: a member of a Turkic ethnic group that originated in central Asia.

Union of Soviet Socialist Republics (USSR): a large nation in eastern Europe and northern Asia that consisted of 15 member-republics. It existed from 1922 to 1991.

United Nations: an international organization formed after World War II whose primary purpose is to promote world peace through discussion and cooperation.

West Slavic nation: one of the nations to the west of Belarus that was settled by the Slavic peoples of central Europe.

Food offerings cover a table during an Orthodox religious service.

After a day of fishing, a boy shows off his catch.

• *Photo Acknowledgments* •

Photographs are used courtesy of: pp. 1, 5, 8, 9 (left), 10, 13 (left), 16 (top and bottom), 18 (right), 19 (top), 20 (bottom), 21 (top), 24, 26, 32, 33, 34 (top), 36 (left), 37 (bottom), 41 (left), 48, 51, 53, 55, © Yury Tatarinov; pp. 2, 6, 9 (right), 17, 18 (left), 20 (top), 21 (bottom), 22 (top and bottom), 23 (left and right), 31, 37 (top), 44, 52, 54, Jeff Greenberg; pp. 12, 13 (right), 34 (bottom), 38, 41 (right), 42, 45 (bottom), 47, NOVOSTI / SOVFOTO; p. 19 (bottom), Rubey Erickson; p. 27 (left), Independent Picture Service; p. 27 (right), Lithuania Research and Studies Center; p. 28 (left), Balzekas Museum of Lithuanian Culture; p. 30 (left), Prints Division, The New York Public Library, Astor, Lenox and Tilden Foundation; p. 30 (right), American Red Cross; p. 36 (right), AP / Wide World Photos; p. 40, © Lynda Richards / Images; p. 45 (top), Belarus Machinery, Inc., Milwaukee, WI. Maps and charts: pp. 14–15, 46, J. Michael Roy; pp. 28–29, 50, 51, Laura Westlund.

Cover: (Front) © Yury Tatarinov; (Back) Dr. Jan Zaprudnik